How to draw MANGA
NINJA WARRIORS

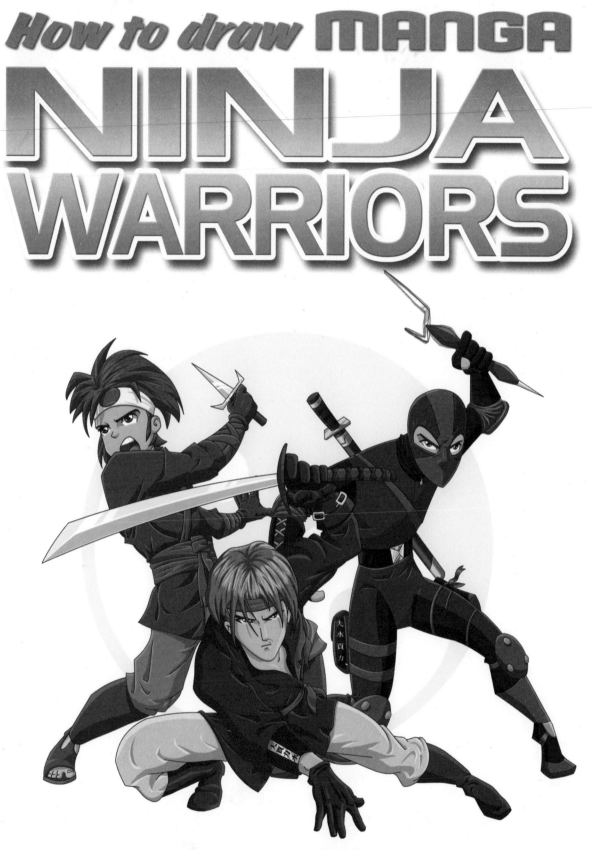

TOPTHAT!kids™

Copyright © 2005 Top That! Publishing plc
Tide Mill Way, Woodbridge, Suffolk, IP12 1AP, UK
Top That! Kids is a trademark of
Top That! Publishing plc

D0335387

WELCOME TO MANGA

Manga is a style of drawing that started in Japan. In Japanese, manga means 'comic book'. In the English speaking world, manga is now used as a general term for all comic books and graphic novels that come from Japan.

Manga became popular in the 19th century, when the comics of a Japanese artist called Hokusai were published for the first time. Hokusai's style of drawing was very different from the manga we have today. Over the years, his style was mixed with others from around the world to create the manga we now all recognise.

Making Manga

In Japan, manga artists are called mangaka. All mangakas have their own drawing style, but there are some style points that you'll see in all types of manga. For example, most manga characters have large eyes, which are drawn to show many different emotions.

Silent Storytelling

A lot of the storytelling in manga comics is done through the expressions on the faces of the characters and the positions of their bodies. By carefully combining expressions and body positions, manga artists can make their characters show emotions such as happiness, anger, fear and sadness without the need for any words!

Meet the Ninjas

Many manga comics are about the ninjas, a special type of warrior. Ninjas were Japanese fighters with special skills and powers. To become a ninja, warriors had to go through years of preparation and practice in special ninja training schools.

Ninja Training

Ninja training included using a wide variety of weapons and learning lots of fighting styles. Their training also taught them how to move quietly and remain still for many hours at a time. These abilities made ninjas perfect spies and secret warriors.

Get Drawing

This book will teach you how to draw different ninja characters in the manga style. So, are you ready to become a mangaka? Then turn the page!

TOOLS OF THE TRADE

Watercolour Tubes

Poster Paints

Waterproof Black Ink

Dip Pen

Eraser

Technical Pen

Thick Brushes

4B Dark Pencil

Medium Brushes

Mechanical Pencil

Fine Brushes

2 mm Mechanical Pencil

2B Solid Graphite Pencil

BASIC FIGURE

Before you start to draw the ninja characters, it is important for you to be able to draw the human figure. Here are the basic steps for a simple standing figure, but first a quick look at proportions.

Male and Female Proportions

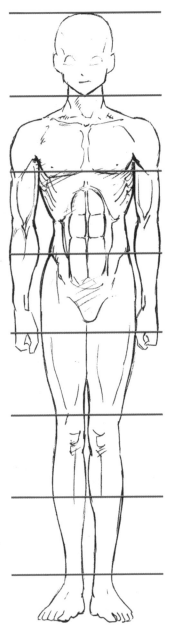

Artists measure human bodies in 'heads'. As you can see above, the body is seven and a half 'heads' in height. Remembering this simple rule will make all the characters you draw look just right.

Female characters usually have narrower shoulders and wider hips than male characters. The female body is slimmer than the male body. Also, muscles are normally more clearly visible in male characters.

Start all your poses with a stick figure to help you
get the position of the body right. Then gradually
flesh out the body, adding the body shape and details.

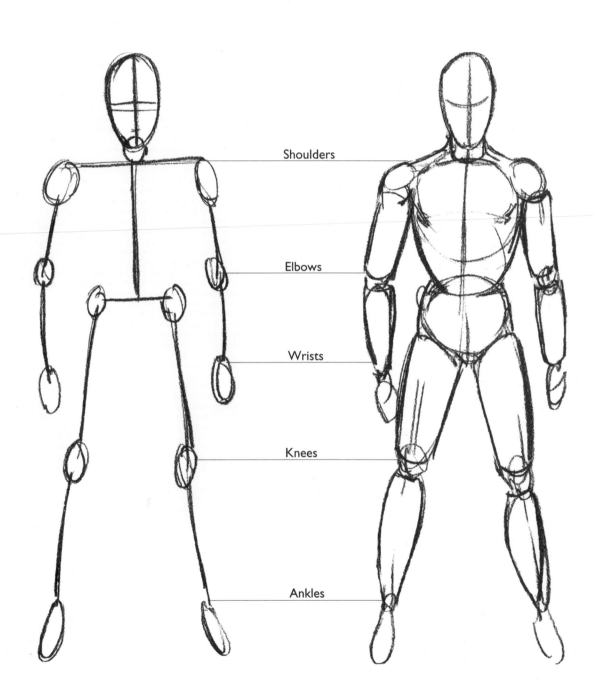

Shoulders

Elbows

Wrists

Knees

Ankles

For a basic stick figure, draw a straight line for the spine. Add more lines for the rest of the body. Use oval shapes to show the position of the head, feet and hands. Use circles to mark all the joints as above.

Now, flesh out the body. Use curved lines and shapes to draw separate body parts such as shoulders, arms and legs. Use an upside-down triangle with curvy sides for the chest and a big circle for the stomach.

character poses

It is important to plan the pose of your character before you start drawing it. Think carefully about what the character is doing and how the body will look. Then follow the same stages as for the basic standing position.

Add the hair and details such as eyes, mouth, nose and ears.

Flesh out the waist to make a full torso.

Add details to the hands and feet.

Flesh out the body around the joints.

To finish a pose, add detail such as the hairline and join all the body parts together. Then add the clothes and weapons. Finish the face, hair and hand detail. When you're happy that your drawing is finished, rub out the guidelines. Now you can add colour.

Look through books and magazines to get ideas for poses and how to draw them. Always try to imagine what the body shapes look like under the clothes. The more poses you are able to draw, the more lively and exciting your ninjas will be.

7

The eyes

Eyes are one of the most important features in manga drawings. They show the feelings of the character and are usually wide and round. Here we show you how to draw a basic eye and a manga eye, so you can see the difference.

Basic Eye

 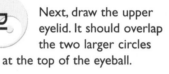 

1. For a basic eye, first draw a circle for the eyeball. Then add two smaller circles inside each other. Colour in the smallest circle.

2. Next, draw the upper eyelid. It should overlap the two larger circles at the top of the eyeball.

3. Finally, draw the lower eyelid to complete the eye. Add finishing touches, and you have a basic eye!

Manga Eye

1. First, draw two curved lines to show the top and bottom of the eye.

2. Now draw an oval that overlaps the line at the top, but doesn't touch the line at the bottom.

3. Add a few pencil strokes for the upper eyelid. Add another curved line above it. Make the oval outline darker.

  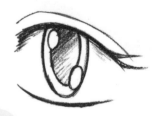

4. Add another smaller oval inside the first one to make the pupil.

5. Add two smaller ovals, as shown, for the highlights. Add some pencil lines for the eyelashes.

6. To finish, add shading to the pupil and remove any unwanted lines. Leave the highlights white and you're done!

Types of Manga Eye

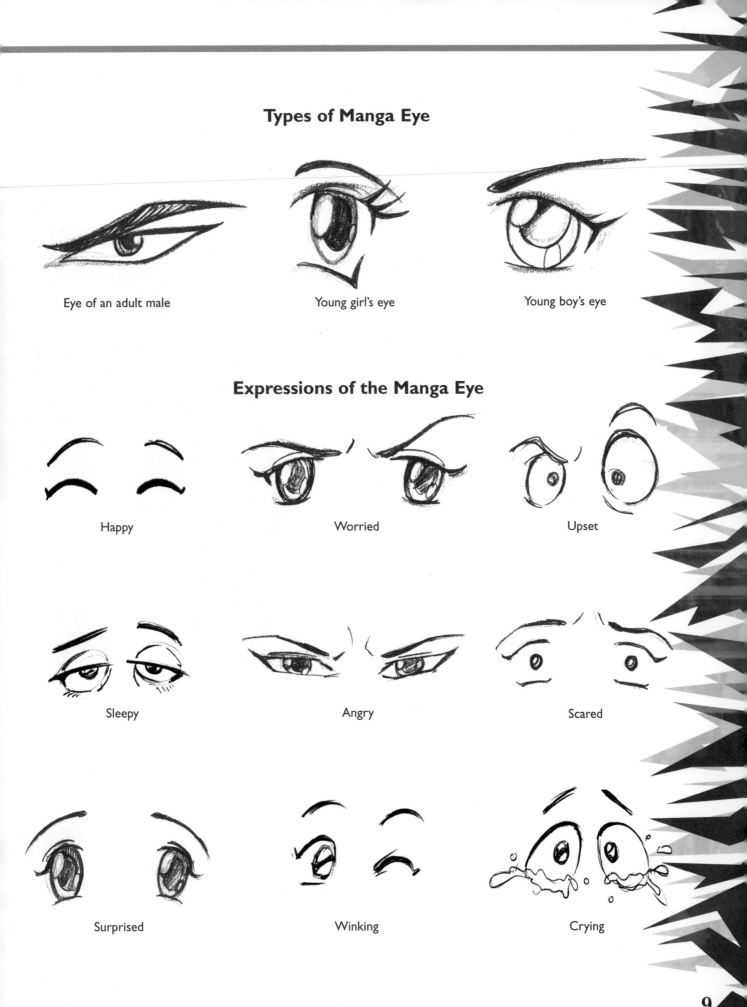

Eye of an adult male

Young girl's eye

Young boy's eye

Expressions of the Manga Eye

Happy

Worried

Upset

Sleepy

Angry

Scared

Surprised

Winking

Crying

MANGA HEAD

Drawing the manga head might seem difficult, at first. However, once you've learnt the basic rules, you'll see it's not so hard...

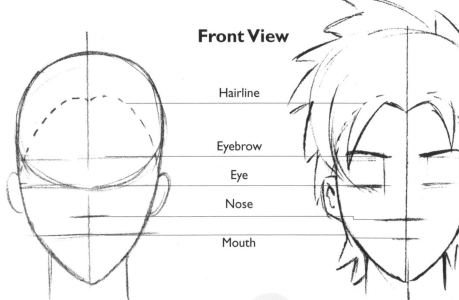

Front View

Hairline

Eyebrow

Eye

Nose

Mouth

1   Draw an oval shape for the head, pointed at the chin. Draw a straight vertical line to divide the face into two. Draw lines across to show the position of the eyes, nose and mouth. Draw a dotted line to mark the hairline. Sketch in the ears and neck.

2   Next, sketch in the position of the eyes and eyebrows. The distance between the eyes should be equal to the length of one eye, which is about 3 cm. Draw in the general shape of the hair.

3   Now, add detail to the eyes, nose and mouth. The eyebrows should be solid shapes. Add lines for the nose and mouth. Smooth the outlines of the hair and add some detail to the ears.

4   Add the finishing touches. A manga mouth is drawn with two lines, one for each lip. Add highlights to the eyes and detail to the hairstyle. Rub out the guidelines and you're done!

Side View

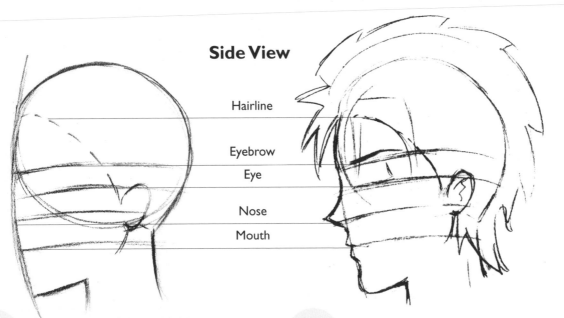

Hairline

Eyebrow

Eye

Nose

Mouth

1 Draw an oval shape for the head, with a point at the bottom for the chin. Show the position of the eye, nose and mouth with horizontal lines. Sketch in the ear and neck. Mark the hairline with a dotted line.

2 Next, sketch in the shapes of the eye, nose, mouth and chin. Draw the shape of the hair. When seen from the side, the manga nose is sharp and points slightly upwards, as shown here.

3 Now add detail to the eye. The eye should be about one eye width in from the front of the face. Notice that the hair follows the shape of the head. Add some detail to front of the hair.

4 To finish, rub out your guidelines and add final touches to your drawing. Remember to draw the mouth line. For most males, the hair ends where the head meets the neck, just below the ear.

11

The hand

Ninjas are masters of many different fighting styles. This includes fighting with just their bare hands. Therefore, it's very important to be able to draw your ninja's hands well. Here, you will learn how to go from stick figure to finished hand in three easy steps.

1 First, draw a basic stick hand. Use a square for the back and add lines for the fingers. Show the joints with small circles. Notice the joints are not in a straight line.

2 Now flesh out the hand by drawing the outlines of the fingers and join them to the palm. Add the shape of the thumb.

3 Finally, add details such as fingernails and short lines for the knuckles. Think about how you can use the same stick figure to draw the palm of the hand.

TOP TIP

Do not use straight lines when drawing hands. Using curved lines will make your hands look more real.

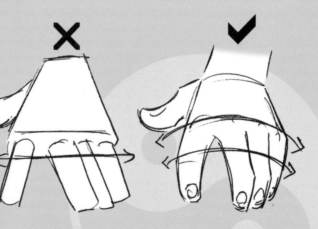

✗

✓

INCORRECT

CORRECT

12

Now that you have the basics of how to draw
hands, look at pictures of hands doing different
things, and practise drawing them.

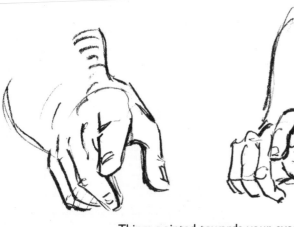

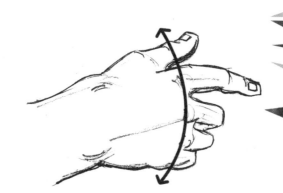

Things pointed towards your eyes
look short, such as this finger.

Notice how the knuckles are curved.

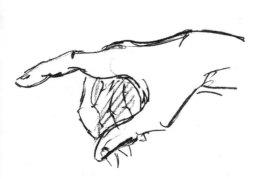

Watch how people use their hands every day,
on the way to school, at the shops and at home.

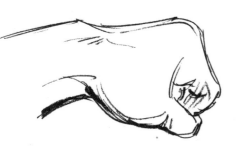

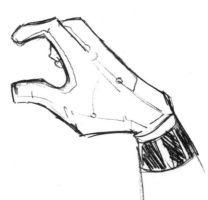

13

The Foot

You will sometimes want to draw your ninjas with bare feet, and many ninjas wear sandals. So here are some simple step by steps for drawing feet.

First, draw an outline of the foot using simple shapes. Use a circle to show the ankle joint and lines to show the toes.

For a side view of the foot, draw simple shapes. Use a line to show roughly where the leg joins the foot.

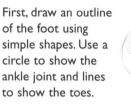

Draw lines for toes

Next, flesh out the foot. Use small tube shapes for the toes. Notice how the toes get smaller. Flesh out the leg.

Make the leg more solid and join it to the foot properly at the ankle. Shape the back of the foot and the heel. Add the big toe.

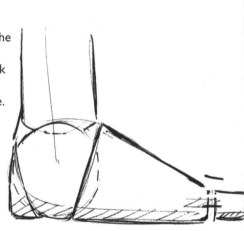

Add circles for toenails

Join the leg to the ankle. Rub out the guidelines. Use thin, straight lines to draw in fine foot bones. Finish the toenails add some shading and you're done!

Add shape to the front of the foot, the ankle, the toes and the heel. Rub out the guidelines. Pencil in the ankle bone and toenail.

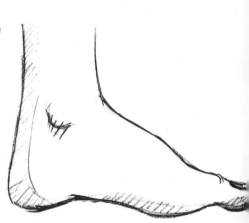

Look at pictures of feet and at your own feet. Notice the different shapes they make in different positions. Also, notice how footwear follows the basic shape of the foot.

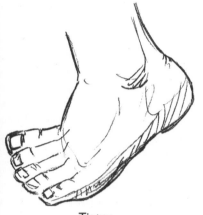

Tiptoe

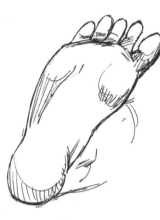

Foot base

TOP TIP

Use fine pencil lines to add details to the feet, such as the ankle bone. Use a thicker pencil to draw in toenails.

Add thick and thin pencil lines for shading.

Dark Shading

Light Shading

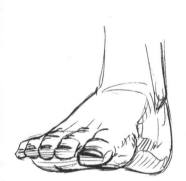

Front foot

Heel

Here we have put shoes on the bare feet. Think about the shapes that have been used to make the footwear. Draw some shoes of your own.

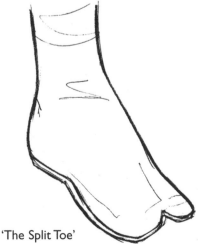

'The Split Toe' ninja shoe

Take off

15

EXPRESSIONS

You can make your manga character show different emotions by changing the way you draw the eyes, the eyebrows and the mouth. By changing these features your characters can look angry, surprised, happy or anything else you want! Here are a few examples.

To make your character look angry, give him an open, yelling mouth. Draw thick downward pointing eyebrows, and square eyes with a thin line under them.

To show surprise draw your character's eyebrows pointing upwards. Give him big round eyes, and a small open mouth.

Closed eyes curved upwards, along with upward pointing eyebrows and a smile show happiness or pleasure.

To show anger or determination, give your character downward pointing eyebrows and narrow eyes. Make his mouth a short straight line, with one corner slanting downwards.

To show displeasure or deep thought, draw the eyebrows pointing downwards. Draw closed eyes curved down, and draw the mouth as a short downward curve.

To show shock or dismay, draw wide eyes slanted upwards. The eyebrows should point upwards too. Give your character an open mouth.

To show your character thinking pleasant thoughts or remembering nice things, give him slightly upward pointing eyebrows and long, thoughtful eyes. A slight smile completes the look.

To show slyness, give your character thick, downward pointing eyebrows and narrow eyes that are looking to one side. A thin, cold smile completes the look of someone planning something unpleasant.

DAN

Fellow ninjas call him 'The Whisper'. Although ninjas are normally very quiet, Dan is exceptionally so. He is a stealth fighter. His favourite weapon is the katana – a Japanese longsword. Dan was very young when his parents were killed by evil warlords and now they are his sworn enemies. He is always there to save an innocent life.

1 Draw a stick figure to work out where the head, body, arms and legs should be. Use circles to show the joints of the body and the position of the arms and legs.

2 Now, flesh out the body. Draw curved lines to show the bulk and position of the different parts of the body.

3 Next, draw the clothes. Notice how his clothes follow the lines of his body. You can also draw his tonfa – a wooden club with a handle.

4 Finish your drawing by adding details such as Dan's eyes, belt, the straps on his boots and, of course, his trusty sword. When you have finished, rub out the guidelines.

 Finally, add colour! Since Dan is a master at hiding, colour his clothes so that he will not be seen when he's tracking the evil warlords.

TAI-CHI

Ninjas are strong fighters and Tai-Chi is no exception! That's a nunchaku, or nunchuk, in his hand. Most ninjas don't use the nunchaku but Tai-Chi is no ordinary fighter. Apart from ninjutsu, this quick-as-lightning ninja has been trained in several other martial art techniques, like kung-fu, karate and judo.

1 First, draw a stick figure to work out where the head, body, arms and legs should be. Use circles to show the joints of the body and the position of the arms and legs.

2 Now, flesh out the body. Draw curved lines to show the bulk and position of the different parts of the body.

3 Next, draw Tai-Chi's clothes. Notice how his clothes follow the lines of his body. Give him his nunchaku, his favourite weapon, which he can use against any other kind of weapon.

4 Finish your drawing by adding details such as Tai-Chi's eyes and the straps on his tabi boots. When you have finished, rub out the guidelines.

5 Finally, add colour! To help Tai-Chi hide in the shadows where he waits for his enemies, give him dark-coloured clothes.

GUNG-HO

Meet the unmasked one! This guy is a cool but totally unconventional ninja. He is known as Gung-Ho by his ninja family, and fights with his bare hands. That's right, this ninja doesn't believe in weapons. Then again, look at him! Does he seem like he really needs weapons?

1 First, decide on the pose you want. Draw a stick figure to work out where the head, body, arms and legs should be. Use circles to show the joints of the body and the position of the arms and legs.

2 Now, flesh out the body. Draw curved lines to show the bulk and position of the different parts of the body.

3 Next, draw Gung-Ho's clothes. Notice how his clothes follow the lines of his body. Draw in his amazing ponytail. Since Gung-Ho doesn't use weapons, be sure to get his powerful fists right!

4 Finish your drawing by adding details such as Gung-Ho's eyes, his wide-open mouth and his belt. Notice how much bigger the left fist is because it's coming straight at you! When you have finished, rub out the guidelines.

5 Finally, add colour! Gung-Ho likes to disguise himself as a street acrobat, so give him bright clothes that will attract the crowds.

TARPAN

Tarpan looks like an ancient warrior. One of the early ninjas, Tarpan is wild and completely fearless. He can also be very dangerous, so beware!

1 First, draw a stick figure to work out where the head, body, arms and legs should be. Use circles to show the joints of the body and the position of the arms and legs.

2 Now, flesh out the body. Draw curved lines to show the bulk and position of the different parts of the body.

3 Next, draw Tarpan's clothes and sketch in his hair. Notice how his clothes follow the lines of his body. Tarpan is very fond of his special sword and shield, so be sure to draw those too!

Finish your drawing by adding details such as Tarpan's eyes, his headband, his armour and the design on his shield. When you have finished, rub out the guidelines.

 Finally, add colour! For Tarpan, use colours that go with his ancient traditions and beliefs, such as browns and blues. He would hate bright colours!

PIKER

Piker is one of the deadliest ninjas around. His name sends shivers down the enemy's spine. Since his family was killed in the last battle with the warlords, he has been angry with everyone and everything. Even his fellow ninjas are careful not to anger him.

1 First, draw a stick figure to work out where the head, body, arms and legs should be. Use circles to show the joints of the body and the position of the arms and legs.

2 Now, flesh out the body. Draw curved lines to show the bulk and position of the different parts of the body.

3 Next, draw Piker's clothes and hair. Notice how his clothes follow the lines of his body. Don't forget his knife, or sai. It might look small, but in Piker's hands it's a deadly weapon!

4 Finish your drawing by adding details such as Piker's eyes, his sandals, his wrist straps and the design on his headband. When you have finished, rub out the guidelines.

5 Finally, add colour! Piker likes to disguise himself as a farmer, so give him bright but cool coloured clothes.

SAMO

Samo is the ninja of the future. He believes in changing with the times – and this shows in his choice of clothes and weapons. He is heavily armed with all kinds of weapons. His favourites, however, are the shuriken, or throwing weapons.

1 First, draw a stick figure to work out where the head, body, arms and legs should be. Use circles to show the joints of the body and the position of the arms and legs.

2 Now, flesh out the body. Draw curved lines to show the bulk and position of the different parts of the body.

3 Next, draw Samo's clothes. Samo wears a futuristic outfit that is like a second skin. Sketch in Samo's sword and the shuriken he is holding. Also, give him elbow and knee pads to protect him during acrobatic fighting moves.

4 Finish your drawing by adding details such as Samo's eyes, his belt, his gloves and his mask. Add pouches on his thighs, where he keeps his shuriken. When you have finished, rub out the guidelines.

 Finally, add colour! For Samo's futuristic clothes, use dark colours like metal grey and steel blue, to help him hide from sight so he can surprise his enemies!

chinc-i

Ching-I is the baby of his ninja family but don't be fooled by his size. This little ninja-in-training is swift and packs a powerful punch. He has been trained to be a super swordsman and can use these weapons to lethal effect!

1
First, draw a stick figure to work out where the head, body, arms and legs should be. Use circles to show the joints of the body and the position of the arms and legs. Note the strong curve of the spine and left leg.

2
Now, flesh out the body. Draw curved lines to show the bulk and position of the different parts of the body.

3
Next, draw Ching-I's clothes. Notice how his clothes follow the lines of his body. Don't forget to give Ching-I his trusty sword.

4 Finish your drawing by adding details such as Ching-I's eyes, his belt and his sandals. When you have finished, rub out the guidelines.

5 Finally, add colour! Since Ching-I is still in training, give him white clothes. As he is already a pretty dangerous ninja, give him a black belt!

NIKO

Ninjas are believed to be deadly killers but this isn't true for all of them. Niko is a perfect example of a ninja with amazing self-control. Niko uses his combat skills only for self-defence and to save lives.

1 First, draw a stick figure to work out where the head, body, arms and legs should be. Use circles to show the joints of the body and the position of the arms and legs.

2 Now, flesh out the body. Draw curved lines to show the bulk and position of the different parts of the body.

3 Next, draw Niko's clothes and hair. Notice how his clothes follow the lines of his body. Niko is specially trained to use the no-dashi – a sword that can be as long as a grown man!

Finish your drawing by adding details such as Niko's eyes, his hair, his headband, his sandals and the hilt of his sword. When you have finished, rub out the guidelines.

Finally, add colour! Since Niko is always looking on the bright side of things so give him colourful clothes and flaming hair!

Keiko

Female ninjas, or kunoichi, are not very common, but that doesn't mean there aren't any. Keiko is one of the most dangerous fighters ever. In fact, she's considered one of the fastest ninjas in the world. The shuriken and the neko-te (iron claws) are the only weapons she needs to fight the bad guys.

1 First, draw a stick figure to work out where the head, body, arms and legs should be. Use circles to show the joints of the body and the position of the arms and legs.

2 Now, flesh out the body. Draw curved lines to show the bulk and position of the different parts of the body. Remember that female characters normally have narrower shoulders than male characters.

3 Next, draw Keiko's clothes and hair. Notice how her clothes follow the lines of her body. Draw her shuriken and the glove that hides her neko-te.

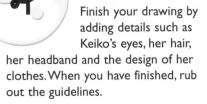 Finish your drawing by adding details such as Keiko's eyes, her hair, her headband and the design of her clothes. When you have finished, rub out the guidelines.

 Finally, add colour! Keiko loves to wear bright colours, so choose some specially for her and give her a cool hair colour!

TARO

Taro is also known as the sailor ninja. He spent many happy years working on his father's trading ship, till the warlords attacked the ship and killed all the men on it. Only Taro survived. Since then, he has dedicated his life to fighting against the warlords and protecting the innocent.

1 First, draw a stick figure to work out where the head, body, arms and legs should be. Use circles to show the joints of the body and the position of the arms and legs.

2 Now, flesh out the body. Draw curved lines to show the bulk and position of the different parts of the body.

3 Next, draw Taro's clothes and hair shape. Notice how his clothes follow the lines of his body. Taro's favourite weapon is his seaman's sword, so draw that too!

4 Finish your drawing by adding details such as Taro's eyes, his hair, his headband, his belt and the hilt of his sword. When you have finished, rub out the guidelines.

5 Finally, add colour! Taro still wears his sailor's clothes and the captain's glove he inherited from his father. So give Taro some strong, deep colours, in memory of his sea-going days!

AJTO

Aito is a health freak. He works out three hours a day and lives on a low-calorie diet. Pumping iron, swimming and sword-fighting are just some of the favourite pastimes of this ninja. He definitely has the muscles to show for it!

1 First, draw a stick figure to work out where the head, body, arms and legs should be. Draw circles to show hands and feet and the joints of the body.

2 Now, flesh out the body. Draw curved lines to show the bulk and position of the different parts of the body.

3 Next, draw Aito's clothes and hair. Notice how his clothes follow the lines of his body. Aito loves his weapons and is never without his sword.

4 Finish your drawing by adding details such as Aito's eyes, his mask, his headband, his belt and the design on the scabbard of his sword. When you have finished, rub out the guidelines.

5 Finally, add colour! Aito loves to show off his powerful muscles, and wears bright colours that draw attention to him.

39

JONIN

He is simply known as Jonin, or 'high ninja', among his followers. A master of weapons and martial arts, he is the leader of the ninja warriors. The mere mention of his name is enough to make the baddest bad guy tremble with fear!

1 First, draw a stick figure to work out where the head, body, arms and legs should be. Draw circles to show hands and feet and the joints of the body.

2 Now, flesh out the body. Draw curved lines to show the bulk and position of the different parts of the body.

3 Next, draw Jonin's clothes and helmet. Notice how his clothes follow the lines of his body. Sharp as a sword and fierce as a tiger, Jonin is a master no one can beat.

4 Finish your drawing by adding details such as Jonin's eyes, hair, gloves, belt, sandals, and the hilt of his sword. When you have finished, rub out the guidelines.

5 Finally, add colour! Jonin is a traditional master, so he dresses in traditional ninja clothes. Give him dark grey or black robes, dark mask and a white belt – and he's ready for action!

COLOURING

Now that you've learnt how to draw your characters, let's find out about the different techniques you can use to bring them to life with shading and colouring.

To use a pencil to create dark areas, you'll need to draw lots of thin lines close together. You can see examples on this character's shoulder, under his chin, and near his ears.

You can build up shading using a technique called 'wash'. Mix black ink or paint with water to make a thin colour or 'wash'. Brush this on the area you want to colour. Let it dry. Mix more black paint with water and put this where you want the picture to be darker. Build up the black like this. Always leave the paper to dry before you add the next layer.

You can use coloured pencils to make light and dark areas using the same technique as above. To make the highlights, leave the paper blank or rub out the pencil.

Watercolour wash is done in the same way as greyscale, but using a single colour. Mix a colour with water and add it to your drawing in layers.

If you're using poster colours, mix the colours with a little water and paint them straight on to the paper. Let the paint dry each time before you add more colours.

You can also use a computer to colour you drawings digitally. Ask your parents or your computer teacher about this.

shading figures

If you want your drawings to be really good, an important point to keep in mind is the light source, or where the light is coming from. This will decide where the shadows in your drawing should be. Well-drawn shadows will make your characters more lifelike and give them depth.

From the Left
In this picture, the light source is coming from the left of the character. Therefore, notice how most of the shadows are along the right side of the ninja's face, hair, arms and body.

From the Top

When the light source is coming from the top of the figure, shadows fall straight down, and are usually lighter. Notice this under the ninja's nose and under his chin. Also notice that the shadows in this case are a lighter grey than in the other two examples.

From the Right

Here, the light source is coming from the right. Notice how most of the shadows are along the left side of the ninja's face and hair. Also, notice the thickness of the shadows near his ear.

ACCESSORIES

It's not much fun drawing ninjas without weapons, is it? We don't think so either. So, here is a selection of amazing weapons you can use to equip your ninja.

Utility Belt
An important part of most ninja outfits, this belt contains small items like shurikens, smoke-making weapons, poison and other secret essentials ninjas don't want the world to know about.

Nunchaku
This simple yet powerful weapon is very useful in one-to-one combat. It takes a lot of skill, speed and training to use it properly.

Ninja Spike
This pouch contains three metal throwing spikes. The pouch can be wrapped around an arm or a leg.

Shuriken
The shuriken – or ninja throwing weapon – can be of many different shapes, such as stars, discs or spikes. They are such deadly weapons that their use has a special name – shurikenjutsu. Masters of shurikenjutsu hardly ever need any other weapons.

Kama
Normally used by farmers to cut grain, this tool becomes a deadly weapon in the hands of a ninja. It is usually thrown at great speed.

Sword
The katana – or ninja sword – is an incredible weapon that can cut through almost anything. Many ninjas use the scabbard of their katanas as a breathing tube, to sneak up on their enemies under water.

Boots
Ninja tabi boots are made for speed, comfort and silence.

Ninjas prefer to keep their identities a secret. You will hardly ever see a ninja without a mask.

First, tie a headband around your ninja's forehead, to keep the hair out of his eyes.

Pull on the hood to cover his head. Finally, pull up the mask, to hide everything but your ninja's eyes!

CLASSIC POSES

What better way to end this book than with some exciting ninja action poses?

Attack!
What will he use?
The knife, his bare hand
or the raised knee?

Defend!
Eyes wide, weapons
ready, weight on toes,
ready to jump in
any direction!

Attack!
In mid-air, sword-point
swinging at the enemy!

Defend!
Do what you dare!
This ninja is ready
and waiting!